INVERNESS REMEMBERED

The Inverness Courier

New Century
Publishing Group

The photographs shown in this book were sourced from
The Inverness Courier's archives, Highland Council Photographic Archive and the
members of public listed below.

Mrs I Herod, Mrs W Macadam, Mrs W Mackenzie, Mrs K Gibb, Mr R Martin, Mrs M
Martin, Mrs C Cumming, Mrs P Pieraccini, Mr M Maclean, Mrs C Morrison,
Mr C Pieraccini.

We would like to thank everyone who has helped us with this publication with which
we have tried to be as historically accurate as possible.
Sincere thanks are due in particular to Mr Syd Atkinson for his valued contributions.

CONTENTS

"A Peek Into The Past"

ALMOST unrecognisable today, that's what you'll discover with many of the scenes we've reproduced for you in this second edition of Inverness Remembered.

In some instances, that is a good thing; in many it can be argued successfully that it is not actually the case.

But whether you see the changing face of Inverness and the way of life of our people as 'progress' or not, one thing's for sure, you'll find some of the faces and places in this volume are a fascinating record of Inverness and the surrounding area in times gone by but mostly within the living memory of our 'more mature' readers.

A PEEK INTO THE PAST

Development of post-war Inverness was rapid and intense. The establishment of the North of Scotland Hydro Electric Board, improved transport links and the setting up of the Highlands and Islands Development Board all contributed to the economic and industrial growth. Coupled with the increased presence of national retail outlets, it resulted in the loss of that 'burgh' atmosphere and the eventual evolution which led us towards the creation of our 'new century' city.

But Inverness has retained many of its best values and there is still a distinct desire to maintain cherished standards around the city and its environs. Folk still care about their neighbours, treasured traditions continue and Invernessians offer a friendly and welcoming environment to visitors and incomers.

Nostalgia apart, what we have recorded on the following pages shows that we have a recent history to be proud of.

"Our Changing Shopping Habits"

Changes in the way we shopped took a significant turn in 1926 with the arrival of the first 'international store' to open in Inverness, F W Woolworth & Co. The firm announced, in a half-page advertisement in the Courier that it would be open for business on the morning of the 11th, listing about 20 different categories of goods that would be on sale and, in large, heavy type, declared: 'The 3d and 6d Stores. Nothing in these stores over 6d'.

The 'goodies' on sale must have proved quite a temptation. There was a mention of the store in the Police Court reports of May the following year. An elderly lady was prosecuted for shoplifting. Apparently she was totally bemused by the glittering attractions spread out on the counters. She said she had no recollection of stealing but would plead guilty. She could hardly have done otherwise since 21 items were found in her possession for which she had no paid. She was fined a pound by Baillie William Michie The value of the 21 items stolen – a total of only 1 shillings!

Increasingly thereafter, the 'multiple shops' – thos owned by limited companies as opposed to famil businesses – arrived in the town. In October of th same year, the Maypole Dairy Company proudl announced that it had just opened its 1000th sho after 40 years of trading. The Dundee Equitable Sho Company, William Low, grocers and Hipps, tailor were early comers to Inverness High Street also.

But, while enjoying the arrival of the new stores Invernessians continued to love and support, thei 'local' businesses, some of which we have recorde in the pictures that follow.

The junction of Hamilton Street and Eastgate, Inverness in the 1950s. The scene there is much changed today with the site now providing a home for part of the Eastgate shopping centre. The Plough Inn, also now demolished, can just be made out on the right of the picture while Mario's is on the left.

Copyright of Highland Photographic Archive, Inverness Museum and Gallery.

OUR CHANGING SHOPPING HABITS

Academy Street, probably post-World War II, given the registration of the cars which, before 1937, had the prefix AS, with AST coming into use after that. In the picture we can see the exterior of Burnetts (see also pages 112/3), the entrance to Macrae & Dick (see also page 107), then Gordon's ladies' outfitters and finally Gilbert Ross the ironmonger.

Carsons dress shop in Union Street, photographed possibly in Coronation year, 1953, given the bunting and crests above the window.

A window display at Lipton's store in High Street in the 1950s. The difference in window dressing from today's preferred technique is quite remarkable. It seems absolutely as much as possible was packed into windows to try to offer 'something to catch the eye of everyone'. Now, the preference seems to be for one or two main items aimed at attracting the line of sight.

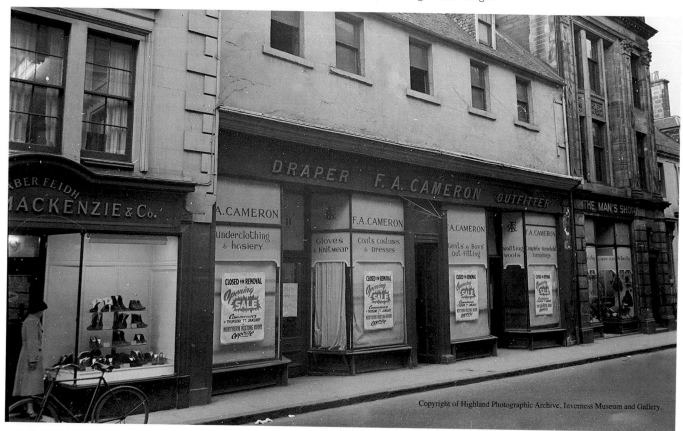

The family business of F A Cameron was long prominent on the retail scene in Inverness. Here notices in the windows indicate the drapers' and outfitters' premises on Church Street was on the move – and that a grand opening sale was to be held across the road at the Northern Meeting Rooms.

OUR CHANGING SHOPPING HABITS

The shop front of Louis Gavin, jeweller and watchmaker in the High Street. His son took over the business. Also in the photograph is the Maypole Dairy. The photograph was probably taken just before or after World War II.

Dorando's Café in Church Street, a chocoholics' dream. This lovely little café specialised in very fancy, top quality chocolates so anyone who wanted a specail treat for themselves or a gift for friends headed to the premises run by Bianco Turriani.

Yes, it even happened in the 1950s. Queuing for retail bargains is nothing new! This is Union Street, Inverness, and ladies eagerly awaiting the opening of The Fashion Salon's first day of sale. The Fashion Salon was run by the Morris brothers and, until it closed, by a wonderful lady called Bessie Morris who had founded it with her husband, Louis.

──OUR CHANGING SHOPPING HABITS──

Copyright of Highland Photographic Archive, Inverness Museum and Gallery.

The well known name of Howdens, seen here on the premises the firm ran on the corner of Church Street and Union Street, probably photographed around 1960 before the move to the garden centre site on Telford Street in 1965. That site was established in 1801 as Muirtown Nurseries and was the oldest advertiser in the Courier, first appearing in 1815.

The Telford Street nursery was huge and ran from the Merkinch School area to beyond Fairfield Road, raising trees for Highland estates and providing employment for many local women, weeding the saplings.

Before occupying the Church Steet premises in the 1950s, Howdens had been at 10 Church Street.

A view along High Street in 1954. In the foreground is Wm Low & Company Ltd, A Prentice, tailor, Hepworths and then John Forbes, The House of Woollens. Next, on the corner of Inglis Street is Boots which had arrived on the High Street in the early 1930s. Until Boots bought the corner site, Forbes's had run from the High Street right round onto Inglis Street.

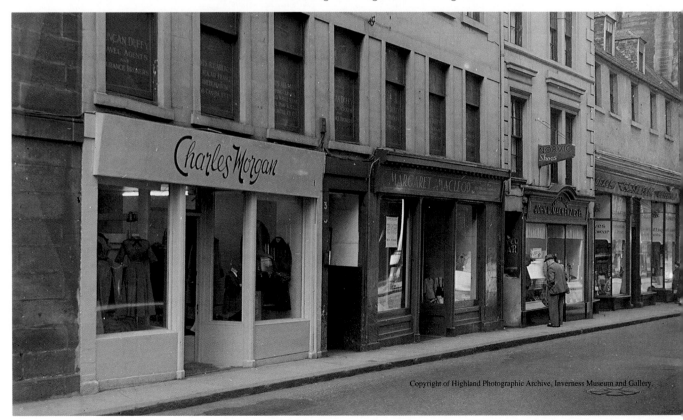

The 'top' of Church Street with a branch of Charles Morgan visible in the foreground. The family business was a prominent ladies' outfitter in the town, with stores at several locations over the years before relocating to the prestigious House of Beauly in 2006.

OUR CHANGING SHOPPING HABITS

Another view of the 'top' of Church Street, this time where it meets Bridge Street.

Among shops visible are Charles Morgan (see also previous page) and John W Mackenzie & Co. Note that there are no parking restrictions. The picture was taken before the redevelopment of Bridge Street and the tobacconist's frontage can be seen at the top. Just off the picture to the left would have been the front of the Town House, the Exchange, and the entrance to Castle Wynd. The junction would have been extremely busy with traffic going in all directions – no one way system in operation then!

15

An early view of the interior of Melven Brothers' bookshop on Union Street, probably from the 1950s.

Duncan Fraser's shop in the market arcade in 1936. The butcher's business has been relocated to Queensgate, where it is still run by the Fraser family, including former Provost William and his son Duncan. As well as being a businessman, William's father, Duncan, was a very well known sportsman in the 1930s and 1940s.

——OUR CHANGING SHOPPING HABITS——

The advent of 'frozen food' brought benefits not only to the households of the Highlands but also provided a boost in economic sectors. And it was not all one-way traffic. Food from the Highlands – vegetables, some soft fruit and meat and game produced here in the north – were frozen and transported south. Here, we see one of the first landmarks of the development of this new style of preserving our perishables, the former Frozen Foods operation on Telford Street.

Grants furniture store on Academy Street was one of the earliest shops in town to sell televisions in the late 1950s.
Here, the window displays seem to be focused on lamps and lighting however.

The corner of High Street and Castle Street which was dominated by A Cameron & Co's department store but now the site of a burger chain.

Copyright of Highland Photographic Archive, Inverness Museum and Gallery.

The firm of Benzie & Miller Ltd on Union Street. Benzie & Miller was a North-east operation which bought over the former Young & Chapman business, a local company owned and run by John Young whose son was a Scottish champion sprinter.

Ian C Young ran in the Empire Games and held the Scottish 100 yards sprint record.
This picture was possibly taken in the 1950s or early 1960s. The store later became House of Fraser and Arnotts before closing down in 2004.

OUR CHANGING SHOPPING HABITS

John Menzies & Co's store on the High Street. There was also a kiosk at Inverness Railway Station. Menzies was the only firm permitted to have bookstalls on Scottish railway stations.

"Entertaining Ourselves"

For several decades, the Empire, the Playhouse and La Scala were our much-loved places c entertainment. All three have now disappeared from our skylines – the final one to close being L Scala in January, 2001.

But it was not just the professionals who could put on a great show, members of our communitie produced some polished public entertainment also.

The auditorium and stage of the Empire Theatre, photographed from the back rows of the balcony. The Empire opened on Academy Street after the Theatre Royal on Bank Street burnt down on March 17, 1931. Will Fyffe was performing at the Theatre Royal that week and, having lost all his clothe and props for his sketches in the fire, travelled immediately by train to Edinburgh to replace them and was back on stage the next night in what had been until then the Central Hall picture house, a special licence having been rushed through for the 'live' performances. The show must go on!

ENTERTAINING OURSELVES

The grand interior of the Empire Theatre, taken from the stage. The Empire provided an extremely popular home for live performances of varying types in Inverness from 1931 until it was demolished to make way for the British Telecom building on Academy Street in 1971.

Some of the brightest stars of the local amateur variety scene who entertained in Merkinch School Hall in January 1939. Among the artistes was Lisbeth Davis, known as 'the schoolgirl ventriloquist' (pictured front right). She was one of the big successes of variety entertainment of the time. In the centre of the picture is Baillie D G Fraser who acted as chair for the event. The concert was in aid of the Inverness District Queen's Nursing Association funds.

Another group of the artistes who took part in the concert in Merkinch School Hall in 1939 to raise funds for the Queen's Nursing Association (see also previous page). The girls were pupils of Miss Olive Cameron and were (from left to right) Betty Inkster, Charlotte Linton, Ethel Inkster, Nina Greenwood and unknown. Also in the picture are thought to be two of the Tolmie brothers, Jock on the left and George on the right. There were four Tolmie brothers, who all took part in theatricals.

The New Caledonian Dance Band, about to head out of Inverness for a 'gig' in September 1938. Standing in the doorway of the bus is Bert Valentine, pianist and leader. The bass player is Johnny Munro the sax player next to the trumpet player is thought to be Bert's brother Willie and the other saxophonist is Bobby Phinn. The trumpet player was possibly Pat Petrie who played in Bert Inglis' (Roberto Inglez) Melody Makers at the Oakwood Roadhouse at Elgin in the mid 1930s. It could be that the drummer, on the left, is Eddie Main, who took over the Melody Makers after Bert Inglis went to find fame with Edmundo Ros in London.

For many years, not only was the Empire Theatre the hub of entertainment in the Highland capital but much of its success was due to the efforts of its manager, the legendary John Worth. Here, John is pictured with some chorus girls at Inverness rail station.

Girls rehearsing, possibly for panto, at the Empire Theatre. Pantos, although sometimes staged by a national company, recruited local young ladies as well. There were several successful dance schools in Inverness, including those run by Alice Grant, Dorothy Macandie, Evelyn Ross, Connie Ross and, around the same time, Olive Cameron. After the war, Sheila Ross (later Mrs Fred Kelly) became a dancing teacher and possibly the highlight of her career was when one of her pupils, Donald MacCleary, won a scholarship to the Royal Ballet School and then became a leading dancer, choreographer and ballet master to the Royal Ballet.

George Robert Wiseman who entertained by playing not only drums but also his musical saw from the 1940s until his death in 1981.

Roddy (Tootsy) Stewart, well known doorman at La Scala cinema on Strothers Lane, standing outside the builiding.

ENTERTAINING OURSELVES

Exhibition dances were extremely popular for a time in between the 1930s and 1950s. National champions were brought to Inverness to give demonstrations of 'modern' dances. In fact, so popular was this pastime that the Inverness Courier ran a column in the 1950s called 'Dancing for Dancers'. This exhibition took place in the Caledonian Hotel, one of the most popular local venues.

It is thought that the young lady second from the left in this photograph is Miss Isabel Bethune. Miss Bethune was an outstanding violinist and while at Inverness Royal Academy was the first winner of the Caird Scholarship for Music. She studied at Glasgow and London, becoming an Associate of the Royal College of Music at an early age and then became a teacher at Glasgow College of Music as well as a recitalist, broadcasting frequently. Although Miss Bethune's family lived in Inverness, it is unlikely that the other ladies in the photograph are local.

"Transportation"

Road, rail, sea and air – all have seen momentous transformation in the latter half of the century just past.

Visitors to Inverness today would probably find it hard to comprehend that the aerodrome in the 1950s and early 1960s was at the Longman, now covered by a sprawling and busy industrial estate.

The roads infrastructure has altered significantly, with one of the major changes being the opening of the A82 trunk road along the north shore of Loch Ness in 1933 and another being the construction of the Kessock Bridge to carry the A9 north across the Inverness Firth in the early 1980s. Still, progress has not been considered to have gone far enough, with repeated calls for the dualling of the A9 and A96 to help improve journey times to and from the south and east and for increased use to be made of the rail network once more to transport freight to Inverness.

The harbour also has seen changing fortunes in the economic map of Inverness. Not many fishing boats tie up at the quays these days. Instead, the harbour has developed through landings and export of petroleum products, timber, salt and coal, along with the continued export of grain and Sterling board. Ships have increased in tonnage and there are ambitious plans for a multi-million pound expansion of the harbour and development of a marina.

Horse-drawn milk floats were a common site around the streets in the 1950s. Here, milkmen load up their transport outside Stratton Dairy's depot in Waterloo Place.

The Eilean Dubh, the popular ferry to ply her way across the Kessock narrows before the building of the Kessock Bridge, is seen here on a summer day, probably in the 1960s. The Eilean Dubh could carry eight cars on the crossing from Inverness to North Kessock on the Black Isle.

The view seen from the Eilean Dubh as she headed for North Kessock (see also above).

Here again, Eilean Dubh crosses from North Kessock (see also previous page).

A Robertson Transport lorry unloading at the quayside at Inverness Harbour – not quite as busy a place as it is today but a vital link for the economic health of the area at the time.

TRANSPORTATION

Another photograph of Robertson's (see also previous page). Note the Inverness phone number only required three digits at that time. Eventually, D Robertson & Son was run by former rally champion, Dan Robertson.

A busy scene at Inverness Harbour in the 1960s. Fishing boats take up the foreground with larger cargo vessels behind.

Another image of fishing boats – sprat and herring drifters – tied up at Shore Street, this time taken in March 1967 – at one time a very common sight at the harbour, with dozens tied up alongside each other in winter, but no more.

Dalcross in 1967 – times have surely changed! The RAF left Dalcross in about 1960 so this picture was taken not long after it became a public aerodrome. The airport moved to Dalcross from the Longman with the arrival of larger planes as the town site was too dangerous to allow them to take off and land safely.

Not much snow clearing on roads and pavements in the 1950s. Coming down Bridge Street onto Bank Street on days like these must have taken some skill behind the wheel.

Bunchrew Station, which served the North and West rail lines from 1862 until it closed in 1960. At the time of the photograph the station was still in operation.

Delmore Road House and Shell Filling Station, at Bruichnain on the Inverness to Beauly road, pictured on a wintry day in the 1950s. The properties sat at the roadside on what was a much busier route at the time – the A9 north before the construction of the Kessock Bridge.

The Road House, probably built in 1936, was quite distinctive in appearance; a rectangular, flat roofed concrete building with a large covered veranda at the front. During World War II, it was an officer canteen and club where Annette Mills, sister of Sir John Mills and famou for playing piano on the children's television show, Muffin the Mule o BBC, came to perform. The idea of roadhouses became popular in th 1930s. They were usually a few miles outside a town and it was commo place to drive out to them for drinks and dances.

A Burnetts delivery van in 1955, a well recognised sight in the town for decades. See also page 122/3.

A delivery van for Hays, the well known house furnishers of Church Street. The picture was taken around 1962.

The Caledonian Canal at Tomnahurich with Zulu drifters in full sail.

An impressive line-up of lorries outside Bon Accord's premises in Inverness. The company had a soft drinks depot at Anderson Street and was run, latterly, by the well-known Robb family of Inverness.

"Sporting Days"

Sporting activities have considerable importance to the people of Inverness who have given wholehearted support to their local clubs, individuals and teams – possibly no more so than in recent years when we have been able to follow our sporting heroes on the world stage.

Much credit must go to local curlers Fiona MacDonald, Janice Rankin and Ewan MacDonald for bringing international glory back to the Highlands in Winter Olympic and European placings while Inverness Caledonian Thistle have wowed us all with their rise to the Scottish Premier League.

But, in the true spirit of sport, no matter what level of accomplishment, or indeed none at all, enthusiasm is always the victor in the Highlands.

Copyright of Highland Photographic Archive, Inverness Museum and Gallery.

Curling at Inverness Ice Rink in November 1968. The Inverness Curling Club has a long history, dating back to 1889.

Inverness Bowling Club at Bishop's Road in the 1930s. The custom was to have an official opening day to the season when the provost of the time was invited to bowl the first bowl. It was a grand occasion.

An Inverness Royal Academy rugby match of 1982-83.

A half-time pep talk during an Inverness Royal Academy rugby match in the early 1980s.

Clachnacuddin FC were the guests of honour at the opening of the new Coronation Park at Avoch in 1953. Clach were one of the original teams to play in the Highland Football League and are still regularly high up the league table at the end of each season, including being league champions in 2003/2004.

The presentation of the winners' trophy. The Lilywhites obviously ran out the winners as the trophy is being handed to club president, George B Rodgers. Mr Rodgers was the man credited with Clach's success between the early 1930s and late 1970s, during which time he took them to their dizziest heights.

Copyright of Highland Photographic Archive, Inverness Museum and Gallery.

Throughout the last century, until the amalgamation which brought about Inverness Caledonian Thistle FC in 1994, Inverness Thistle Football Club had its home at Kingsmills Park and provided Highland football with many important sporting memories. Here, Roy Latham is pictured at training, keenly watched by young fans, no doubt hoping to pick up some tips for a successful future in the game.

SPORTING DAYS

Inverness High School hockey team of 1934.

The Inverness Caledonian football team at Dalcross before flying to Stornoway in 1953. From left to right are Willie Jack, Donald 'Ginger' MacKenzie, Ernie Fraser, David Forrest, Alasdair Chisholm, John McFadyen, Donald Morrison, Willie Jamieson, 'Stootie' Fraser, Willie Bruce, Bobby Bolt, Dan Lowry, Dave Birrell and George Munro, a Caley President in the early 50s and whose son Brian is also well known to all as the present editor of the Caley Thistle programme.

39

Inverness Royal Academy shinty team of 1948-49.

Inverness Royal Academy shinty team of 1949-50.

SPORTING DAYS

Inverness Thistle on the attack while playing against Aberdeen FC. Thistle, established in 1888, played in the Highland League, but not Aberdeen, which would indicate Thistle had probably won the qualifying cup and taken on the Dons in the Scottish FA Cup. The other possibility is that this was a pre-season friendly but the crowd looks too large for such an occasion.

Highland Hockey Club six-a-side team.

"Our Way Of Living"

Fashions and hairstyles may change but one thing never alters, our interest and amusement when looking back on the way we used to live – our habits, pastimes, values, employment and how we spent our schooldays.

Here, we bring you a snapshot of Invernessians in the 1940s, 50s and 60s – and some even from the 30s.

Are summers really hotter now? Well it looks like it was a scorcher on this day in the 1950s as these two lasses try to cool off.

Agricultural life played an important part in the economy of Inverness. The Northern Counties Show, held at the Bught Park, was a popular occasion, particularly for folk from outlying areas to come into town, not only to do a bit of business but also to meet up with friends and socialise.

Inverness Royal Academy prefects of 1948-49, pictured with rector, the legendary D J MacDonald.

43

An intriguing school photo from Inverness Royal Academy in 1953. What on earth was the play? We seem to have a sailor, Jacobite, Britannia, a fairy, a witch, an elf – and possibly a mad hatter or two! The age range is also interesting.

An Inverness Camera Club outing. Is this the 1950s?

Miss Jean MacDonald outside the Locarno Café. The Locarno stretched from Academy Street right through into the old Victorian Market and was owned by well known and much respected Renzo Serafini. It was a great meeting place for Invernessians and out of town folk.

Jean MacDonald behind the counter of the Locarno Café in 1961. The Locarno boasted one of the biggest ranges of bottled sweets in the Highlands. (see also above).

Children pictured outside Farraline Park School in the 1930s, probably shortly before it closed in 1937 when the children were transferred to Crown Primary. The impressive Greek Revival-style building had opened as a school in 1841. It now houses Inverness Public Library.

7th Coy Boys Brigade. Back – Donnie MacAskill, Evan Lumsden, Chas MacKenzie, Doc MacKenzie, Ally MacGruer, Jackie Panton. Front – Ally MacAskill, Don Baddon, Don MacLennan, J Gillespie, J Skinner.

Silver Service waitresses at Drumossie Hotel.

Inverness High School hockey team. Mary Lumsden, unknown, Frances Fraser, Ann Skirra, Elma Maclean, Isobel Kennedy, Margaret Maclean, unknown, Rachael Douglas, unknown, Joyce Rattray.

Class of 1959 at Inverness High School. This photograph has been kindly supplied by Mr MacPherson of W D MacPherson & Sons, outdoor clothing specialist in Inverness. Some familiar faces in the picture include Mr MacPherson himself, Ella MacRae of Dores Inn – and now a local councillor – and Willie MacLennan. Also pictured is Miss MacKay, mathematics teacher and depute head of the school.

Massed pipe bands marching through Inverness in June 1950.

The 6th Company Inverness (St Mark's Church) Boys' Brigade pictured in 1954.

A gauger (excise officer) doing checks at Millburn Distillery.

Win MacKenzie (nee Hay) being presented with a goodie bag by John MacMahon. Mr MacMahon, a landowner and estate agent, was a prominent citizen in the town. He was well known for two things in particular, his generosity, along with his brother, in annually donating gifts to local schoolchildren and being three times commended for saving the lives of people who had fallen into the River Ness. Here, he is pictured with Councillor Frank Rizza (dark hair) and Central School janitor Mr Munro (in cap). In the background, by the school entrance is headmaster Mr W S Shaw.

Headmaster of the newly built Inverness High School, William S Kerr, pictured in front of the building in 1937, the year after it opened. Also in the picture are thought to be councillors Alexander Carfrae, Andrew Cameron and William Macintyre. The men of the cloth are the Rev Richard Rae Beckitt of St John Episcopal Church (left) and the Rev Kenneth Cameron of the Free North Church.

William S Kerr, headmaster of Inverness High School, possibly with a large group of teachers pictured some time in the late 1930s.

The annual Boy Scout and Girl Guides Church Parade on Sunday, May 15, 1938. The companies assembled in front of Farraline Park School and marched to the Old High Church for an afternoon service via Inglis Street and High Street with Provost Hugh Mackenzie taking the salute.

The Guides leaving Farraline Park School to march to the Old High Church pass the gates to the playground and No 17 Margaret Street, the Jannie's house. The school, on the top right, had closed the previous year. (See also previous page)

Fourteen year old Arthur Bright of Mitchell's Lane, in Scout uniform, shakes the hand of his friend Donald Macpherson, of 15 Ardconnel Street. Both boys were members of St John's Troop and had gone to Lochend on April 11, 1938 to do some climbing. While scaling a difficult rock face, Donald slipped and fell. It was thought at first he was seriously hurt and Arthur revived him with water from a nearby stream before helping him to a woodman's hut half a mile away and then going for assistance. The injuries turned out to be not too severe however and Donald is pictured here thanking his friend and rescuer. The other children are Arthur's brother and sisters.

A security check at Kessock Ferry in 1940. Such checks were one of the irritations of wartime living that became very familiar in early 1940. Under the Defence Regulations, practically all the Highlands and Islands north and west of a line from Inverness to Oban became a Protected Area and no one except residents, children under 16 and Forces personnel could enter without a permit. But the pass arrangements were said to be 'chaotic'!

Miss Catherine (Kate) Reid had a ladies and girls outfitters shop at Eastgate in the 1920s and 1930s. She was a founder and later president of the Inverness branch of the Soroptimist movement which was set up in the town in 1935. Also in the picture, is Mrs Helen Kennedy, the first ever lady magistrate of Inverness. The picture was probably taken in 1937 and could have been a meeting of the Inverness branch of the Electrical Association for Women. In the picture are, seated from left, Miss Reid, Miss Macdonald and Mrs Helen Kennedy and standing, left to right, unknown, Miss Molly Ross and Miss Lily Grant.

Playing bridge at a ladies' church group.

Members of Clachnacuddin Cycling Club set off on the second run of the season to Nairn via Ardersier in March, 1938. Not quite as dangerous an undertaking as it would be on the busy roads of the area today.

The latest fashion evening wear.

The staff of the Inverness Courier at an outing to Errogie House, probably pre-World War I.

Young Highland dancers at Coronation day sports at the Bught Park.

Police officers inspecting a float at Inverness auction mart. The float appears to have come from Fort William and it is likely the driver is disinfecting his vehicle as required by law. The officers, carrying out their duties under the Diseases of Animals Acts, are Chief Insector and Deputy Chief Constable William Dalgleish and Constable Alasdair MacBean of the Burgh Police Force and the visit was taking place late in 1937 or early in 1938.

Two 'bouchers' – or 'bowshers' – immobilised by floods in the Ness Islands in the early 1930s. In the 1930s the closure of the Islands due to floods was so commonplace that there were no reports in the Courier of the situation. Only when people's houses were affected did details appear.

Members of Inverness Gun Club on a shoot in 1937, probably including some 'crack shot' gamekeepers from the area.

The opening of the British Sailors' Society Home in Baron Taylor's Street in March, 1940. Pictured here are, from left, Mr H Barker, honorary secretary of the British Sailors' Society, Miss Lucy Cruickshanks, secretary of the local branch, Lady Hermione Cameron of Lochiel, Lord Inverclyde, chairman of the Scottish Advisory Committee of the society, Lochiel KT, Mrs Mackintosh of Drumaline, president of the local branch, the Rev Arthur Hamilton of St Stephen's Church, Petty Officer Morrison, caretaker of the home and Rear Admiral Hervert Pott MVO.

William S Kerr, headmaster of Inverness Technical High School from 1933 until 1953, thought to be receiving a swimming shield won by the four-boy team around him. Handing over the shield to Mr Kerr is William Aikman Hardie, secretary of the Inverness Swimming Club and vice-charman of the Scottish ASA.

The annual ploughing match organised by the Inverness-shire Farmers' Society in February 1937. It took place at Drakies and Beechwood farms, courtesy of the owners, Angus Matheson and the Department of Agriculture. The judges are in the picture and were Alexander Munro of Leanach, Kenneth Paterson of Cantraybruaich, John Fraser of Midmills Road and George Brander of Bogside. Not much ploughing goes on at Drakies or Beechwood now!

Buying the Sunday papers on Academy Street – and, if you were lucky, ice cream as well.

What story lies behind this picture – a son going off to war? It was taken inside Inverness Railway Station in the 1930s.

Culduthel Hospital staff of the 1930s, including Sister Munro, Sister Asher, Edward Vinson, Staff Nurse McHardy and Matron Asher.

OUR WAY OF LIVING

How grand the staircase is in this photograph at the Station Hotel – possibly taken in the early 1960s. Is this an office staff outing?

An entire book could be written about the salmon netting on the Ness. Here, the fisher doalies, as they were known, are seen hauling in a net just off Huntly Street. In the background is the Lord Roberts Memorial Workshops which, after closure as uneconomic, became a furniture depository in March 1958. The building with the chimney is the 'destructor' which burned local refuse to produce electricity and was a source of affection as well as at times aggravation for many Invernessians during the 41 years of its life. Bowlers at the nearby Waterloo club could leave the bowling green grey with soot from the destructor.

INVERNESS REMEMBERED

The fisher 'doalies' hauling in nets which had earlier been taken out on the river by boat.
The salmon trade was an important source of revenue to the town for generations. In the background here is the Black Bull pub.

Scottish weddings have many rituals associated with them designed to bring good luck, or ward off bad. In rural areas, there was a tradition of throwing coins to local children as the 'happy couple' left the church and as time passed, the custom was seen around Inverness also. The bridegroom would dip into his pocket or sporran and throw loose change to the youngsters gathered around.

The hotels along the riverside provided a picturesque setting for a wedding reception.
Here, a wedding party arrives at the Palace Hotel, probably in the late 1950s.

INVERNESS REMEMBERED

In the 1950s plumbed in bathrooms were much more evident than in past decades, particularly in town homes. But large volumes of hot water were not quite so readily available. It was quite common therefore for smaller children to be bathed in the kitchen sink. Some things don't change however – note the 'bathtime duck' played a prominent role in events even then – although this one does have a suspicious look of a dragon about it!
If you were 'posh' enough to have two sinks, the metal strip between them, seen here, was used to hold a clothes wringer in place.

Children, thought to be from the Leachkin area, at a Christmas party in the 1950s.

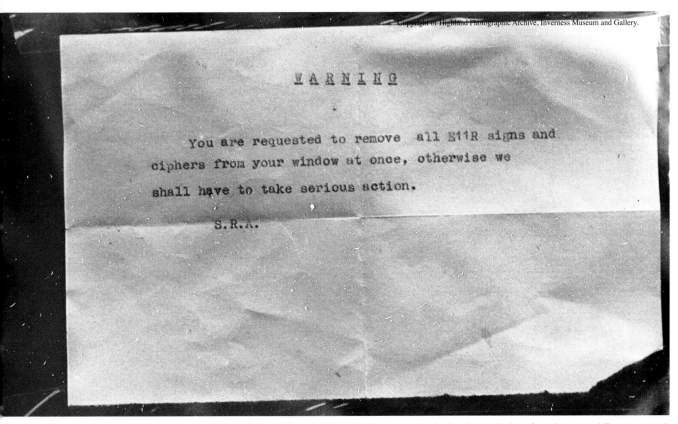

WARNING

You are requested to remove all E11R signs and ciphers from your window at once, otherwise we shall have to take serious action.

S.R.A.

Life was not all harmony in post-war Inverness. A Scottish Republican Army notice threatening 'action' against a display of royal memorabilia was pasted to the outside of Benzie & Miller's store on Union Street prior to the visit of Queen Elizabeth the Queen Mother in 1953.

A line-up of pretty finalists in the Miss Inverness beauty pageant of 1954. Winner was Eileen Williamson (centre back). There was quite a history of such contests after a national newspaper began them in the town in the 1930s and they continued through until well after the war.

Fishermen, probably from Avoch, but on board an Inverness-registered vessel, proudly displaying a shark. It was a relatively rare but not unknown situation to catch a shark in waters off the coast around the Highlands. This one was landed at Thornbush Slipway in the 1950s.

Staff at Raigmore Hospital pictured in 1947. The sprawling buildings on the site at the time were erected to provide wartime emergency care but the hospital units continued to serve the people of the Highlands well until the new towering structure we now know as Raigmore was completed.

Cameron Highlanders at Inverness Airport, possibly the TA. But what was the occasion, or indeed their travel plans?

Inverness Sea Cadets. This is thought to be a group pictured at a tattoo in 1955.

Jimmy Nairn produced a wonderful collection of photographs in and around Inverness in the 1950s. He also had a very fine collection of movie film which, had it unfortunately not been lost in a fire, would have provided very valuable record of life in Inverness. Also much involve with the Air Training Corp locally, remarkably for the time, he constructed a flight simulator where young ATC members could actually go through the motions of flying. Pictured here with Jimmy, is his son.

According to the Highland Photographic Archives, this photograph is of Post Office staff, taken in the Caledonian Hotel ballroom in 1960. Strangely, given the numbers involved in the event, more details have not come to light, despite the photograph being reproduced in the pages of the Courier in May 2004.

A presentation taking place at the function pictured above.

Father George McCurrach, (later Canon) the first parish priest of the 'bright and modern' St Ninian's RC church which was built on Culduthel Road to help house the increasing congregation in Inverness and surrounding area, along with the existing St Mary's.

In the 1940s and 1950s considerable change began to occur across some of the lochs in the Highlands with the introduction, on a grand scale, of the hydro-electric dam system. The projects brought a huge influx of workers to the rural areas involved and benefits to the local economy during construction work. Here, we see the vast Mullardoch dam under construction. One of the dams on the Affric/Beauly system in Glen Cannich, it was completed in 1952. A small power station was built near the south end of the dam and water from the loch was put through a tunnel to feed Loch Beinn a' Mheadhain in Glen Affric and went from there to help feed the huge power station at Fasnakyle, south of Cannich.

A celebratory drink inside one of the massive tunnels on the Invergarry hydro scheme. The workers were known as tunnel rats/tigers and mainly came from Ireland, Europe and, of course, Scotland. They set up their camps on the site of the construction projects and their efforts changed the living conditions of Highlanders forever with every home benefiting from the 'hydro electric'.

Earlier schemes had been set up around the Highlands in the last century, of course, particularly to feed the needs of the North British Aluminium Company – but nothing on this scale.

A tunnel on the Glenmoriston-Garry scheme with some idea of scale being indicated by the gentleman standing on the bottom left of the picture. This section of construction was taking place around 1953.

These massive schemes started after the wartime government appointed the Cooper Committee which recommended the setting up of the North of Scotland Hydro Electric Board. The board's efforts brought about changes not always recognised for their significance today – and not always welcome in the Highlands at the time, with fears of the 'destruction of the beauty of the area'. Now controversy surrounds the activities of the electricity industry once again, with protests over the proposed Beauly to Denny 'super-pylon' project.

"Events"

We all need a little pomp and ceremony in our lives from time to time to help us mark special occasions, give us something to look forward to or, in the case of the aftermath of the royal abdication of 1937 featured in this section, create a bit of buzz and speculation.

Some events are indeed momentous and featured on the 'world stage', such as the loss of John Cobb when his boat crashed on Loch Ness, but others are more of a thrill on a personal level, for example, the first sighting of an elephant walking down the High Street!

Yes, Inverness has 'seen it all' over the years, and coped with whatever challenge was put in front of us.

Kirking of the Council in January 1973. Provost of the time was William Smith and the town clerk was John R Hill. After each local authority election it is the custom that the new council is 'kirked'. The councillors and officials leave the town house, proceed through the streets to the Old High Church for the service and then return to the town house.

The Kirking of the Council in 1973. Is this council officer Charles MacRae leading the procession from the gates of the Old High Church?

The Kirking of the Council in June 1978, this time showing the halbadiers. (see also previous page)

Massed pipe bands marching to the Northern Meeting Park in the late 1950s. The temporary bridge can be seen in the background during the new Ness Bridge construction project. The pipers are probably on their way to the Northern Meeting Park, possibly for the annual Tattoo.

The Queen's Own Cameron Highlanders War Memorial Boys' Club opened in 1953 following a local fundraising campaign which saw generous donations. Membership was open to boys between the ages of 12 and 18 and the objective was to promote the physical, mental and spiritual fitness of boys, to encourage the formation of character, powers of leadership and good citizenship. The club was run by a board until around 1960 when its operation was taken over by the local authority. It continued to run as a boys club and later as a community centre.

His Royal Highness, the Duke of Edinburgh, visiting the Queen's Own Cameron Highlanders War Memorial Boys' Club building in Planefield Road. The idea for such a club originated among members of the QOCH towards the end of World War II and public fundraising began.

A momentous and solemn occasion, Sheriff Principal R H MacConochie reads the Proclamation of the Accession of the Earl of Inverness to the throne of the United Kingdom as King George VI, following the abdication of his brother Edward. The date of the photograph was Monday, December 14, 1937. The Provost of the day was Provost Hugh Mackenzie.

A young whale found washed up on the shore of the firth? It is said to be the Sowerby's whale discovered stranded two miles east of Inverness in July, 1932. The creature was dispatched by train to be studied at the Natural History Section of the British Museum in London. Sowerby's are the most commonly stranded beaked whale and in the mid 1800s, the Courier regularly reported cases of them being stranded or driven ashore. Is it a Sowerby's? Whatever its species, it certainly drew quite a crowd.

EVENTS

The arrival of Santa at Inverness railway station generated much excitement in the 1950s and even into the early 1960s. Santa would travel to Inverness by train – rather than reindeer – to be driven the short distance across Academy Street and along Union Street to occupy his 'grotto' in Benzie & Miller's store.

Almost as popular as royalty or the superstar celebs of today, Santa drew huge crowds on his arrival at Inverness railway station. (see also above)

INVERNESS REMEMBERED

The eyes of the world were on Loch Ness in September of 1952 as Londoner John Cobb set out on his attempt to break the water speed record.

He brought his boat, Crusader to the loch-side and launched his bid. He successfully completed the one mile distance but, to achieve the record, needed to return over the same length so that a 'mean speed' for the two runs could be calculated.

As he accelerated to make the turn, the crowds on the loch shore gasped in horror as Crusader exploded apart. The rescue plan flew into operation – but Cobb was dead.

He had succeeded in his aim of being the fastest man to travel on water, reaching a speed of over 200mph. But his bid at breaking the record could not stand because the challenge had not been completed.

Locals round Drumnadrochit had taken Cobb to their hearts in the weeks leading up to the attempt and after his death raised a cairn to his memory on the loch-side.

Copyright of Highland Photographic Archive, Inverness Museum and Gallery.

Copyright of Highland Photographic Archive, Inverness Museum and Gallery.

Crusader on a trailer before the record attempt. She was 31ft long, built of aluminium and marine ply and was powered by a jet engine. Her remains lie undisturbed on the bottom of the loch.

John Cobb, said to be a big, unassuming man, spent weeks at Loch Ness preparing for this fateful bid at the water speed record. During that time, he encouraged locals, including school children, to visit the base he had set up for his team at Temple Pier and he is still remembered fondly by folk today.

The circus comes to town! What a spectacle Billy Smart's convoy makes as it wends its way into Inverness along the High Street. Today, circus lorries would hardly rate a second glance but in the 1940s and 1950s, crowds lined the streets to greet the travelling entertainers.
Circuses had been coming to the Highland capital from the mid 1800s and were usually the best in the country. Among 'famous names' who appeared locally were Lord John Sanger and Buffallo Bill.

The loudspeaker on the lead vehicle ensured no one missed out on the arrival of the cavalcade.
From the numbers in the picture, however, word must have got around early. (see also previous page)

In the 1950s it was still acceptable to have live animals performing with the circus.
This elephant was certainly cause for some slightly 'cautious' smiles when it stopped outside the Town House.

Always a favourite, the clowns from Billy Smart's Circus give High Street crowds a preview of fun to come.
The ringmaster rides behind to ensure not too much 'clowning around' .
Billy Smart's became incredibly successful with the post-war general public and featured regularly on the fledgling BBC television programme. Televised
Christmas and Easter Circus extravaganzas followed and made Smart's Circus the most famous of all circuses travelling in the UK.
At the height of its powers Billy Smart's Circus toured with a huge 6000 seater big top, an army of international circus artistes, and a 200 strong host of
elephants, lions, horses, polar bears, camels, sealions, and chimpanzees.

Bertram Mills was the most regular circus owner to visit town and usually
brought his impressive big top north by train.
However when he arrived in 1933 travelling via Loch Ness-side, he is
reported to have offered a sum of £20,000 for the capture of Nessie.
Needless to say, no one got the cash!

The Bertram Mills elephant parade crosses the Ness suspension bridge.
When the circus came to town, the keepers fed these stunning animals on
the trees in the Bught and they were taken to the Ness Islands to bathe.

EVENTS

Six-day reliability motor cycle trials attracted a large crowd to the premises of R MacRae & Sons in June 1914. The bikes, which had set out from Edinburgh to attempt various routes round the Highlands, would have been housed overnight in the premises. Note the cobble stones which must have been a challenge to ride over! Much of the organisation for this event's overnight stop in Inverness probably took place thanks to the efforts of the Inverness Motor Club, formed three years previously.

The cow in this picture on the left became something of a legend in the Highland capital and many were not so sure as time passed if the story of its escapades was actually true. However, here is the photographic evidence that it was. The beast was being taken to the marts on Eastgate when it broke loose and, no doubt terrified by traffic, took refuge in the 'Buttercup' on the corner of nearby Hamilton Street where it fell through a flight of stairs on its way to the first floor!
The cow was eventually rescued, but not before it had caused considerable damage to 'Buttercup' stock, as witnessed above right.

83

Is this happy swimmer Margaret Munro? Margaret was famed for her swimming ability and emigrated to Australia. She is the holder of several titles as a national swimmer. If you were a keen swimmer in Inverness, you proved your ability by taking part in the annual Kessock swim. Another to make quite an impression was a young Ian Black who swam over and back when he was still only around the age of nine. Ian went on to become arguably Scotland's most successful swimming champion, bringing many gold, silver and bronze medals home from European and Commonwealth Games.

CHANGING STREETSCAPES AND SCENERY

"Changing Streetscapes and Scenery"

Sometimes, the pace of change seems almost too rapid. We feel a sense of sadness as a way of life disappears or a recognised landmark is threatened with demolition.

When the old Ness Suspension Bridge was replaced, for example, it changed the face of the centre of the town significantly forever. Mind you, it took a while to happen, thanks in the main to the activities of one Adolph Hitler. But with increased traffic volume and weight, there was little option but to replace it with a structure suitable for the 'modern road network' and its demands.

There were plenty of other, more subtle changes, and until you look at the pictures on the following pages, you might not even recall all of them.

INVERNESS FROM THE CASTLE

Inverness, pictured from the castle pre-World War II. Work on the new Ness Bridge began in the early part of 1939 but progress ground to a halt, understandably, during the war years. Difficulty in obtaining government grants continued to keep the project on hold following the cessation of fighting in 1945 and it was not until the late 1950s that work resumed. The temporary bridge intended to be used during the replacement of the Ness span opened just two weeks before war was declared so it lay there in preparation for around 20 years.

85

The part-demolished Ness Bridge in December 1959.

An impressive view of the towers of the old Ness Bridge in 1954.

CHANGING STREETSCAPES AND SCENERY

The Old Ness Bridge with the temporary bridge in front of it, pictured in 1959.

A close-up view of the temporary bridge which was in place during construction of the new Ness Bridge. This appears to be in the demolition stage in 1963, with parts of the guard rails missing. Ropes can also be seen attached to parts of the Oregon pine piers, presumably to help pull them down.

INVERNESS REMEMBERED

Construction continues on the new Ness Bridge in 1960.

An early photograph of Inverness High Street. In the foreground on the right can be seen the Forbes Fountain in its original state. The fountain was offered to the town by local exile Dr George Forbes from his home in India and presented in 1880 when it was placed at the space in front of the town house known as the Exchange. From then until well after World War II there were regular arguments about moving it. Eventually, partly to a[llow] viewing of Queen Elizabeth, the Queen Mother, on her visit to the tow[n] in 1953 it was finally agreed to move it. But this beautiful example of fi[ne] Victorian architecture was smashed and the top wrecked. Now the on[ly] remaining aspect of it, the base, is repositioned at Cavell Gardens.

CHANGING STREETSCAPES AND SCENERY

An early postcard photograph of Academy Street, Inverness, showing just one horse and cart plus a few pedestrians. The corner of Union Street is visible and as that was built in 1870, and Queensgate in the 1880s, it is possible to date the postcard as just before the turn of the century.

Inverness and the river from the castle. In the foreground is the building known as Castle Tolmie, with Queen Mary's House behind.

Another view from the castle. (see previous page also)

The town's old Victorian statues Faith, Hope and Charity can clearly be seen on the top of the former Tartan Warehouse building on the corner of High Street and Castle Street. The building was eventually knocked down to make way for McDonalds and the Three Graces were bought for scrap and taken to Orkney where they are now thought to be in the Graemeshall House private collection of antiques.

CHANGING STREETSCAPES AND SCENERY

An interesting view of Queensgate looking from Academy Street, probably taken in the 1940s,
with the former Royal Insurance building on the bottom right.

Union Street with the old Caley Hotel in the background and a solitary horse and cab, possibly pictured in the 1930s.

The Seaforth Bar, part of the structure of the Caledonian Hotel on Church Street and a favourite with tourists.

Inverness looking east over the river to Bank Street before the demolition of the old Ness Bridge.
The gas works, as well as the steeples of St Columba and the North church, are clear landmarks on the skyline.

CHANGING STREETSCAPES AND SCENERY

A view over the rooftops of Castle Street from the grounds of Inverness Castle. But the homes are not there now – presumably a victim of the landslide which saw a huge mass of earth cascade down from the hillside onto Castle Street below in 1932, carrying houses and the Columba Mission Hall in its wake.

Demolishing the swimming baths in 2001. The baths became redundant when the new Aquadome opened in 1997. The baths opened on July 1, 1936 and saw huge crowds queuing the length of Glebe Street and up Chapel Street to get in. One hundred and thirty thousand gallons of water were pumped into it from the River Ness by two fire engines prior to the opening.

The interior of the swimming pool, commonly known as 'the baths'. One side was for females and the other for males. For many years head pool attendant was the much respected and popular Roddy Dyce, whose way of telling if you had been in the pool too long was to examine your hands and i they were wrinkled, you were out!

The Clydesdale Bank building on the corner of Church Street and Queensgate.

Queen Mary's House was demolished in 1968, although the vaults of the old house were saved and incorporated into the entrance hall of the new Highlands and Islands Development Board building. The house was given its prestigious name after Mary Queen of Scots reportedly stayed there in 1562. She had been denied entry to Inverness castle because of the political situation at the time but her army eventually succeeded in gaining access.

Friars Street with the British Telecom 'exchange' at the top and the Old High Church steeple in the background.

CHANGING STREETSCAPES AND SCENERY

A beautiful snowy scene at Culduthel. This is the former entrance to Culduthel hospital.

Gilbert Street in the 1950s. On the left of the picture is Chisholm's Tannery. In previous times, that area of the town was used as an overnight stop by drovers taking their cattle south. In fact the general area, which is known as the Merkinch, itself translates as 'Horse Island'. The river had several outlets at that area and the Merkinch was indeed an island in times past.

A fine view of Victoria Public Park, a much changed landscape from the one we know today. This is the view from Tomnahurich Hill and shows Park House and Ballifeary Lane on the right. At one time, a bandstand, similar to the one on the links at Nairn, was sited in the centre of the parkland, in front of the tree on the right of our picture. There was a nursery on the left and what is today Maxwell Drive would now more or less dissect the park we see here.

A snow covered Station Square in 1954 before the frontage of the station was redesigned.

CHANGING STREETSCAPES AND SCENERY

High Street in the 1950s or early 1960s?? looking from west to east with Cameron and Co's building in the foreground.

The attractive rose window in the former Wesleyan Church in December 1984. At the time, the first floor was the site of the Stewart Restaurant with the Jacobite Cruise booking office below. The huge stained-glass window was unveiled to much acclaim at the opening of the former Methodist Chapel in 1868 but was removed when the building was demolished in the 1960s. It has lain in storage in local authority care since then awaiting a new site.

Waterloo Place pictured in the summer of 1981.

The junction of Crown Drive with Eastgate in 1977 with Masons electrical store on the corner. Opposite is a glimpse of the Plough bar, a popular local haunt and a busy place on mart days.

A view from the High Street looking down Bridge Street in 1953 – were the flags out to celebrate the Queen's Coronation or for the visit of Her Majesty Queen Elizabeth the Queen Mother to be granted the freedom of the burgh in August of that year?

The entrance to Macrae & Dick's premises on Academy Street in 1980.

Queen Mary's House photographed in 1954. (see also page 99)

James Walker & Co's sawmills in Shore Street. It is likely the photograph was taken around the time of the firm's 75th anniversary in April 1938. The family members and partners in the firm contributed greatly to life in the burgh, including being instrumental in setting up the Highland Orphanage in 1880.

When James Walker & Co opened in 1863, it announced that it was welcoming visits from architects, builders and cabinet-makers and promised moderate prices for 'deals, battens and other scantlings, also floorings, linings, boardings, sarkings, etc which would always be in stock'.

"Our Beautiful Buildings and Landmarks"

Like any town, Inverness has a mish-mash of architecture in places and a few examples of it not that attractive. However, there are also extremely fine, handsome buildings to be proud of and we bring you photographs of some of them on the pages that follow.

Many have been lost over the past few decades of course but, with others, although the street frontages may have changed, by raising the eyes to first floor, second floor or even roof levels, often you are more likely to see the beauty of the original architecture, particularly on town centre streets. Well worth a try.

The original Kingsmills, pictured here in 1958. On the left of the picture is the road running down to Culcabock curling pond and the main junction in the centre of the picture is certainly vastly different today.

Highlands and Islands Fire and Rescue service headquarters in Harbour Road, a very modern building when it opened in the 1950s. It followed considerable debate in the local press about the need for a new fire station to serve the growing population of the town. Before World War II the fire station had been run on a part-time basis from premises on Castle Wynd. The double doors which had been used for the station on the side of the present town house have now been converted into a window but just above, very faint traces can still be seen of the words 'Fire Station'. At the time, when a fire occurred, the horses which normally pulled hackney cabs, would be 'collared' into service. During the war there was an auxiliary fire service station next to Fraser Park but following the war the National Fire Service was established, standardising training across the country.

Display boxes at the entrance to David Whyte's photographic studio on Church Street.
David Whyte's name is still well known in Inverness, although the studio is no longer in business. Mr Whyte came to Inverness during the 1860s and over the following decades many a local family or business had portraiture or commissions undertaken at Whyte's. The works have now been catalogued into a collection.

OUR BEAUTIFUL BUILDINGS AND LANDMARKS

The flats at Coronation Park in South Kessock. Building on the estate began in the 1930s.

Inside Inverness Railway Station concourse in the 1930s. The old booking office is on the right of the picture.
Note also the many advertising hoardings of the time, including for Camp Coffee and Craven Plain cigarettes.

Culcabock Filling Station pictured in the 1930s or 1940s. In the background we can see the Fluke Inn and today Crossways Garage stands on the site just to the right.

The Cumberland Stone, Culloden Moor. The Duke of Cumberland, leading the government forces, was said to have stood on the stone to direct operations during the battle of Culloden in 1746. However it is very doubtful that he ever did in fact stand on the stone to view the battle because he was actually very much in the thick of it.

The Cairn and graves of the clans at Culloden Moor

Leanach Cottage on Culloden Moor, now under the jurisdiction of the National Trust for Scotland but for may years in living memory still occupied by an elderly lady.

"Hotels, Pubs, Eating Out And Entertaining Our Tourists"

At the end of the 19th and beginning of the 20th century, tourism began to play an increasingl significant role in the economy of the Highland capital, helped greatly by the development of the railways.

Hotels were needed, of course, and have continued to be an integral aspect of the livelihood of Invernessians.

Local folk enjoyed themselves going for a dram too, maybe having a game of 'doms' or samplin the fine food on offer at the cafes and restaurants that were increasingly springing up aroun Inverness.

The very grand frontage of the Palace Hotel on Ness Walk. During World War I the Palace was taken over by the navy and was the billet for the senior nav officer for the area. In 1919, questions were being asked in Parliament as to when the Royal Navy was going to vacate the hotel. Apparently, the navy was very comfortable in its Highland home but there was some scepticism as to whether such a 'significant' presence was still required for such an area.

HOTELS, PUBS AND EATING OUT

The reception area of the MacDougall Clansman Hotel on Church Street.
Above the fireplace is the crest of the MacDougall clan, 'Cincere vel mori' – to conquer or die.

very impressive display of alcohol behind the bar of the Criterion on the corner of Baron Taylor's Street and Church Street. The Crit was one of the most popular watering holes in Inverness when this photograph was taken.

The Caledonian Hotel on Bank Street, pictured in 1954. The original hotel was built by local Masonic lodges and for the first years of its life was known as the Mason's Hotel. In front of the hotel car park is the booth for the parking attendant, standing on an area which would originally have been garden ground up until around 1900.

The obviously successful domino team at Stewart's Bar in Union Street. In the centre of the picture is Miss Duncan, the proprietor.

The imposing building of the Royal Hotel in Academy Street. Sadly, it closed and was converted into a branch of the Clydesdale Bank.

INVERNESS REMEMBERED

This picture of the Cummings Hotel on Church Street was probably taken in the late 1930s or early 1940s. On the edge of the picture, on the left, is Bow Court and between the buildings ran a lane to the rear of the Empire Theatre. It was not unknown for performers to nip out of the stage door between appearances on stage, knoc back a 'quick one' in the bar of the Cummings and rush back to the theatre in time for the next act.

A prominent rooftop sign for Conn's Restaurant on Inglis Street. Victor Conn, an Italian gentleman, had a far-reaching vision to bring French cuisine to Inverness an in the 1930s opened the Condor Restaurant which sold snails and frogs' legs. It also had a little three-piece orchestra. But Mr Conn may have been just a bit ahea of his time because that business did not do well and, apparently in his own words, was a 'white elephant'. He also ran other restaurants however, including th one on Inglis Street, and an extremely popular confectionery shop. Other businesses on the street include R S McColl, the Club bar and D Watson, taxidermist.

HOTELS, PUBS AND EATING OUT

Copyright of Highland Photographic Archive, Inverness Museum and Gallery.

This would have been a regular scene in many bars in the 1950s, and still is today in some – men playing dominoes.
Now, the more common pastime in many pubs is viewing sport on giant televisions however.

Copyright of Highland Photographic Archive, Inverness Museum and Gallery.

The staircase of the Station Hotel, probably pictured in the 1930s.
The former coffee room is on the right but the hotel, re-named the Royal Highland, is much changed now.

In all its glory, the fine building of MacDougall's Hotel in Church Street. The MacDougall was one of the very few temperance hotels in the Highland capital. (see also page 115)

The Rendezvous, a popular restaurant on the corner of Ness Walk and Young Street, owned by the Cardosi family from Wick. Just out of the picture to the left was the Ness Cafe, owned The town's old Victorian statues Faith, Hope and Charity can clearly be seen on the top of the former Cameron & Company's building on the corner of High Street and Castle Street. The building was knocked down to make way for McDonalds and the Three Graces were bought for scrap and taken to Orkney where they are now thought to be in the Graemeshall House private collection of antiques. by another Italian family, the Caffrinis.

The famous tearoom of Burnetts Bakery on Academy Street. The Burnett brothers, John and William, said to have cycled to Inverness in 1896 to set up their business, opened their first bakery in Dempster Gardens, with a sales shop in the High Street. In 1907 they bought the Inverness Steam Bakery and shop, part of the Old Academy building. The shop fronted Academy Street with the bakery behind in Strothers Lane. This is the interior of the tearoom on the first floor which became THE place to go for afternoon tea in the town.